How Are Mountains Formed?

B.J. Best

Cavendish
Square
New York

Published in 2018 by Cavendish Square Publishing, LLC
243 5th Avenue, Suite 136, New York, NY 10016

First Edition

Website: cavendishsq.com

This publication represents the opinions and views of the author based on his or her personal experience, knowledge, and research. The information in this book serves as a general guide only. The author and publisher have used their best efforts in preparing this book and disclaim liability rising directly or indirectly from the use and application of this book.

CPSIA Compliance Information: Batch #CS17CSQ

All websites were available and accurate when this book was sent to press.

Library of Congress Cataloging-in-Publication Data

Names: Best, B.J.
Title: How are mountains formed? / B.J. Best.
Description: New York : Cavendish Square Publishing, 2018. | Series: Nature's formations | Includes index.
Identifiers: ISBN 9781502625458 (pbk.) | ISBN 9781502625472 (library bound) | ISBN 9781502625465 (6 pack) | ISBN 9781502625489 (ebook)
Subjects: LCSH: Mountains--Juvenile literature. | Orogeny--Juvenile literature.
Classification: LCC GB512. B47 2018 | DDC 551.43'2--dc23

Editorial Director: David McNamara
Copy Editor: Nathan Heidelberger
Associate Art Director: Amy Greenan
Designer: Alan Sliwinski
Production Coordinator: Karol Szymczuk
Photo Research: J8 Media

The photographs in this book are used by permission and through the courtesy of: Cover Kittikiti/Shutterstock.com; p. 5 Galyna Andrushko/Shutterstock.com; p. 7 pio3/Shutterstyock.com; p. 9 Seaphotoart/Shutterstock.com; p. 11 Webspark/Shutterstock.com; p. 13 Peter Hermes Furian/Shutterstock.com; p. 15 Craig Aurness/Corbis/VCG/Getty Images; p. 17 Armmphoto/Shutterstock.com; p. 19 Radoslaw Lecyk/Shutterstock.com; p. 21 Kastianz/Shutterstock.com

Printed in the United States of America

Contents

Mountains are in many parts of the world.

A mountain is a huge hill made of rock.

Earth is shaped like a ball.

It is made of many **layers**.

7

We live on Earth's **crust**.

It is the layer on the outside of Earth.

The crust is all of the land.

It is also the land under the sea.

The crust sits on a layer called the **mantle**.

The mantle is inside Earth.

It has rock that is melted. This rock can **flow**.

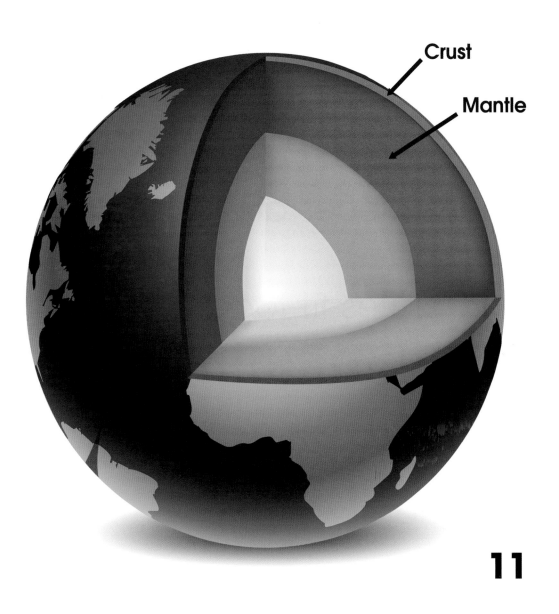

Crust

Mantle

11

The crust is made of huge pieces.

These pieces are called **plates**.

The plates fit together like a puzzle.

The plates move over the mantle.

12

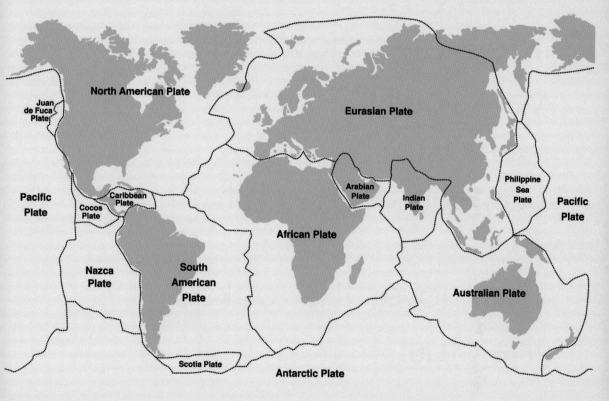

13

The plates move very, very slowly.

Sometimes they hit.

This moves the rocks in the crust.

The plates can crunch together.

This makes a pile of rocks.

This pile becomes a mountain!

17

Small parts of plates can break off.

They can move up or down.

This can make a mountain that looks like a wall.

It takes millions of years for a mountain to be made.

Mountains are still being made today!

21

New Words

crust (CRUHST) The outside shell of Earth.

flow (FLOH) Move like water.

layers (LAY-erz) Levels.

mantle (MAN-tuhl) Some rocks inside Earth.

plates (PLAYTS) Huge pieces of Earth's crust.

Index

About the Author

B.J. Best lives in Wisconsin with his wife and son. He has written many other books for children. He has hiked up a mountain in Alberta, Canada.

About BOOKWORMS

Bookworms help independent readers gain reading confidence through high-frequency words, simple sentences, and strong picture/text support. Each book explores a concept that helps children relate what they read to the world they live in.